???

THE QUESTION COLLECTION

OVER 600 QUESTIONS ABOUT

BOOKS

SPORTS

PEOPLE & PLACES

MATH

SCIENCE

ART, MUSIC, AND MORE

Written by Carol Eichel & Evelin Sanders
Illustrated by Beverly Armstrong

???

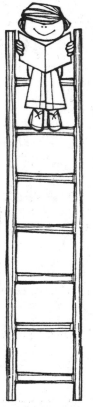

The Learning Works

Edited by Sherri M. Butterfield

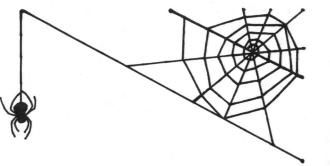

Copyright © 1988
THE LEARNING WORKS, INC.
P.O. Box 6187
Santa Barbara, CA 93160
All rights reserved.
Printed in the United States of America.

Introduction

This book is a collection of more than six hundred questions covering such topics as art, astronomy, famous quotations, geography, government, grammar, history, literature, mathematics, music, presidents, science, space exploration, and sports. It is intended for use in the classroom, at home, or anywhere people have empty minutes to fill, and should be ideal on rainy days, before recess, during parties, or while traveling.

The questions have been arranged four to a page. Questions on any one page cover different topics but are of a similar degree of difficulty. The pages have been arranged within the book so that the questions progress from easy through medium to hard. In general, questions on the first fifty pages should be easier to answer than questions on the last fifty pages.

3

The Question Collection
© 1988—The Learning Works, Inc.

No collection of questions would be complete without a collection of answers. In this book, the collection of answers appears at the back of the book, on pages 171–184. To make needed answers easier to find, they have been listed by page number and keyed by letter to a particular position on the page. Thus, answer **a** is for the question in the upper left-hand corner, answer **b** is for the question in the upper right-hand corner, answer **c** is for the question in the lower left-hand corner, and answer **d** is for the question in the lower right-hand corner. (See diagram.)

a	b
c	d

A Special Message to Teachers

The ways to use this book in your classroom are almost endless. To begin with, of course, you can open it to any page and ask a few questions to fill those last minutes before lunch or recess.

You can turn the questions into a **self-checking game**. Select pages on which the questions are appropriate for the grade level you teach. Duplicate some of these pages and cut the questions apart. Glue each question to one side of a plain index card. Glue or write the corresponding answer on the other side of the card. Laminate the cards and make them available as part of a classroom display or learning center.

The Question Collection
© 1988—The Learning Works, Inc.

You can turn the process of answering the questions into a **research activity**. Select pages on which the questions are somewhat challenging for the grade level you teach. Duplicate these pages and make cards, but do not write the answers on the cards. Instead, write the appropriate page number and answer letter. Distribute the cards, and challenge individual students or teams to find and record the answers within some specified time limit. Then, check their results against the answer key. You may want to keep score on a chart or graph by the week or month.

You can use the questions on a particular topic as part of a **classroom display** on that topic. For example, look through the book and select a group of questions about U.S. presidents. Duplicate the pages on which they appear. Cut out the questions you have selected and post them on a classroom bulletin board or wall. Make blank cards available and suggest that students write and illustrate additional questions on the same topic and add them to the display.

In addition, you can use these questions for question bees, for staged classroom quiz shows that follow a radio or television format, as motivators for students who get bored with routine classwork, and as pleasant bonus activities for students who have completed their assignments and are looking for something more to do.

In short, you may find that The Question Collection provides a lot of answers for a busy teacher in a bustling classroom.

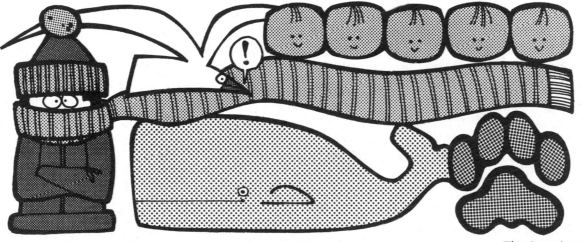

A Special Message to Parents

The ways to use this book are almost endless. To begin with, of course, it's perfect for filling indoor time on rainy days, amusing a child who is ill, or making the miles go faster when you travel. For example, your child might use it to stage a **quiz show** in radio or television format. For a change, let your child be the quizmaster while you play contestant and try to supply the answers.

Use selected questions as a **party game**. Choose teams, ask questions, keep score, and reward the winners with prizes of some kind. Use this book to **sharpen research skills**. If your child does not know an answer, instead of telling him or her, help him or her look it up in a dictionary, encyclopedia, or other similar reference book. Or use this book as the inspiration for an **art activity**. Supply plain index cards and a black felt-tipped marking pen and encourage your child to add to The Question Collection.

Name the three primary colors.

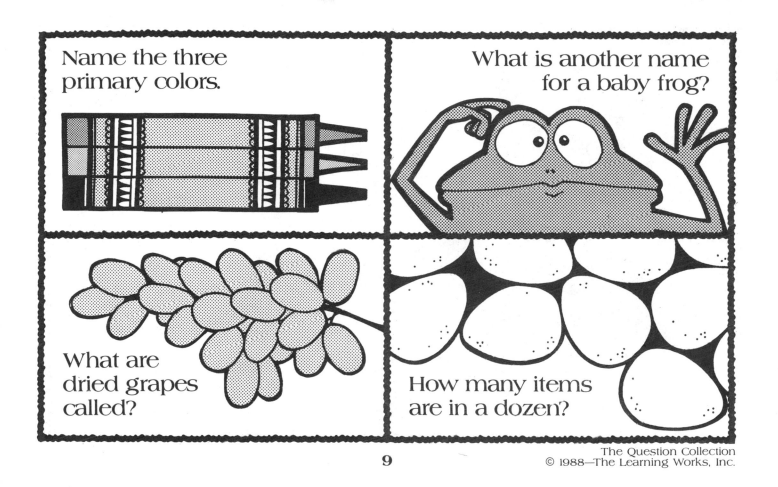

What is another name for a baby frog?

What are dried grapes called?

How many items are in a dozen?

What kind
of tree
has acorns?

What
instrument
is used
to measure
temperature?

Whose picture
is on the penny?

What is a
baby cow called?

What are dried plums called?

In roman numerals, for what does the letter X stand?

How many ounces are in a pound?

JELLY BEANS
NET WEIGHT 4 OUNCES

What is a baby deer called?

The Question Collection
© 1988—The Learning Works, Inc.

A barrier built to prevent the flow of water is called what?

How many inches are in a yard?

What is a book of maps called?

On what ship did the Pilgrims sail to America?

In which country were the first Olympic Games held?

What do the stars on the U.S. flag represent?

Tiny Tim is one of the central characters in which story by Charles Dickens?

Who was the first president of the United States of America?

The Question Collection
© 1988—The Learning Works, Inc.

What name is given to an area of land that is surrounded by water and is smaller than a continent?

Who invented the electric light bulb?

Which is the longest river in the world?

ZZZZZZZ

Which one of Washington Irving's characters slept for twenty years?

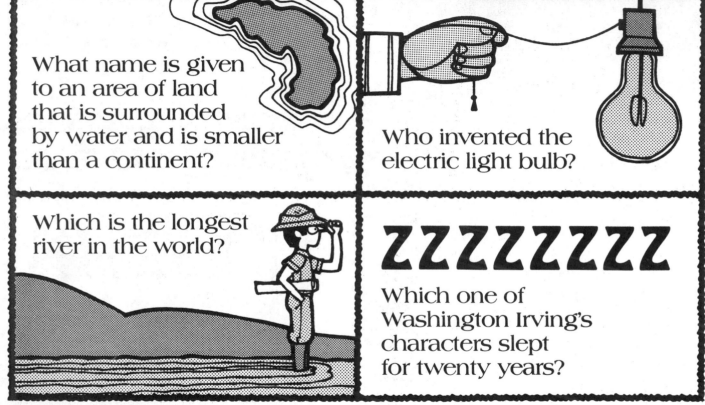

What is an eight-sided figure called?

Name the giant north woods lumberjack who is a hero of American tall tales.

What country lies directly north of the United States?

Who is said to have made the first American flag?

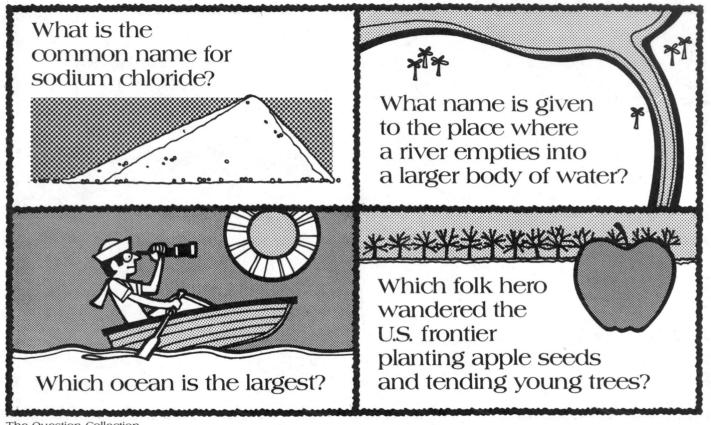

What is the common name for sodium chloride?

What name is given to the place where a river empties into a larger body of water?

Which ocean is the largest?

Which folk hero wandered the U.S. frontier planting apple seeds and tending young trees?

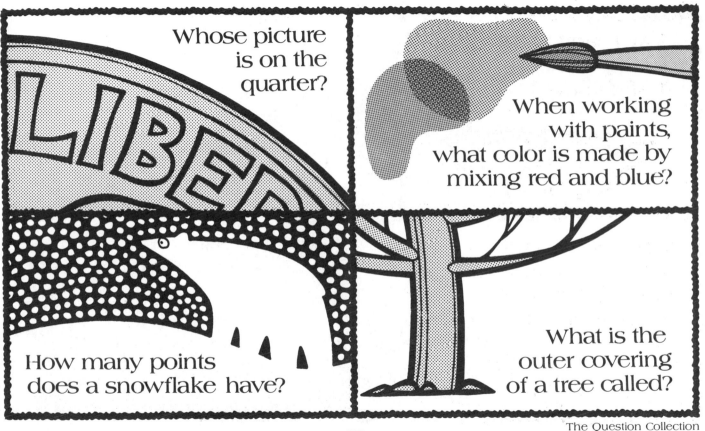

Whose picture is on the quarter?

When working with paints, what color is made by mixing red and blue?

How many points does a snowflake have?

What is the outer covering of a tree called?

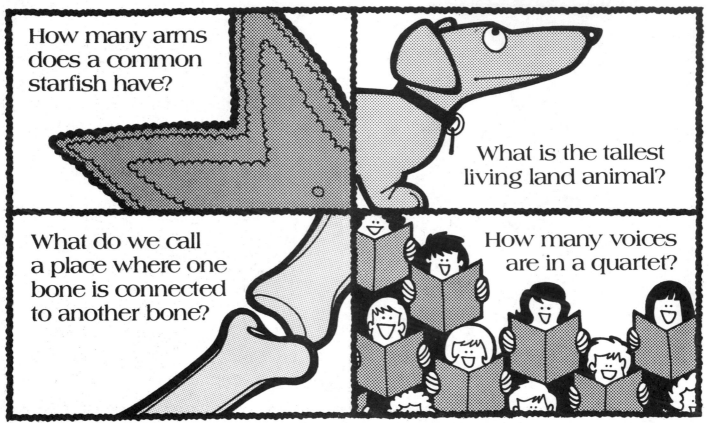

How many arms does a common starfish have?

What is the tallest living land animal?

What do we call a place where one bone is connected to another bone?

How many voices are in a quartet?

What do we call
five babies born
to the same mother
at the same time?

How many
legs does
an insect
have?

In roman numerals,
for what does
the letter V
stand?

V ?

How is your
father's brother
related to you?

19

The Question Collection
© 1988—The Learning Works, Inc.

How many years are in a century?

Whose picture is on the nickel?

What country lies directly south of the United States?

What do we call a violent, whirling wind that is accompanied by a funnel-shaped cloud?

What do the stripes on the U.S. flag represent?

In what year did Christopher Columbus discover America?

Land ho!

When Aladdin rubbed his lamp, what would appear?

What bird is the national symbol of the United States?

21

How many pounds are in a ton?

How many sides does a die have?

When working with paints, what color is made by mixing red and yellow?

A doctor who specializes in treating animals is called what?

Name the fictitious resident of Puddleby, England, who was able to talk to the animals.

What is a group of fish called?

How many pints are in a quart?

MILK

ONE QUART GRADE A

MILK

Which is the longest river in the United States?

23

How many quarts
are in a gallon?

What is a person wearing
if he has on spectacles?

Whose picture
is on the
five-dollar
bill?

In which direction
does the sun rise?

With what do most fishes breathe?

How many sides does a stop sign have?

In which city would you find the Eiffel Tower?

How is your father's sister's child related to you?

Daddy

Me

Aunt Elizabeth

The Question Collection
© 1988—The Learning Works, Inc.

Whose picture is on the one-dollar bill?

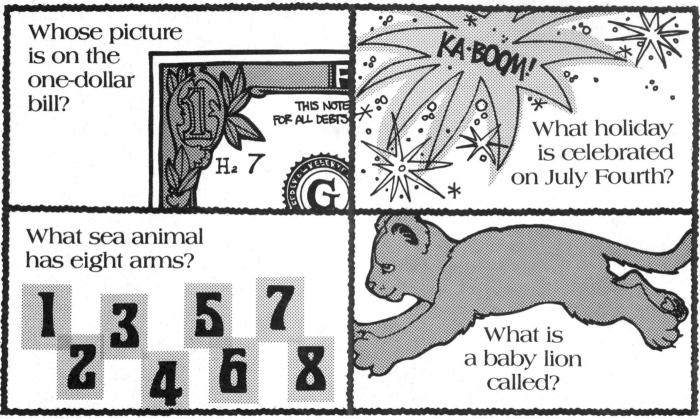

What holiday is celebrated on July Fourth?

What sea animal has eight arms?

What is a baby lion called?

What is a male chicken called?

How long does the earth take to make one complete rotation on its axis?

Of what material are glaciers made?

How many days are in a year?

JANUARY FEBRUARY MARCH APRIL MAY JUNE JULY AUGUST SEPTEMBER OCTOBER NOVEMBER DECEMBER

27

What do we call groups of stars that seem to form pictures in the sky?

What is the color of the highest belt awarded in judo?

puffin

What is a puffin?

What is the chemical formula for water?

Where did Robin Hood and his merry men live?

The process of bringing water to dry land so that crops can be grown on it is called what?

Name the man who used a kite to demonstrate that lightning is electricity.

Which state was the last to join the Union?

Where is the Astrodome?

What other name is given to an Eskimo's canoe?

Mount Vernon was the home of which U.S. president?

Name the boy hero who runs away to Never-Never-Land to escape growing up.

NEVER·NEVER·LAND

What do we call a finger of land with water on three sides?

Who invented the telephone?

In Ernest Lawrence Thayer's famous poem about a baseball game, what "hero" strikes out?

Which ocean lies between the United States and Europe?

U.S.A. • EUROPE

The Question Collection
© 1988—The Learning Works, Inc.

Who was the first American woman to travel in space?

The Statue of Liberty was a gift from what country?

Name the volcano that erupted in the state of Washington in 1980.

Dr. Jonas Salk developed a vaccine against what crippling disease?

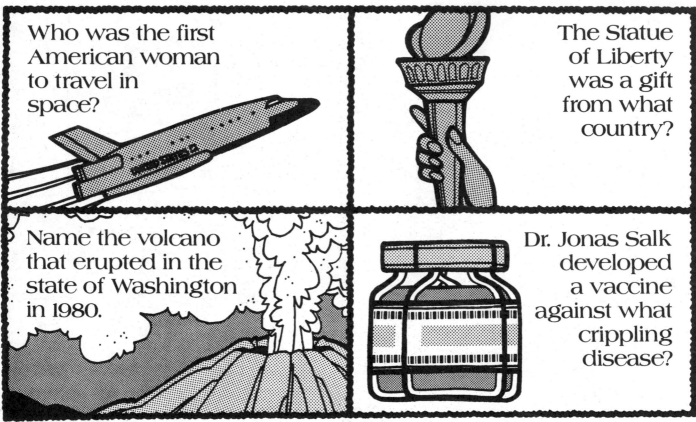

With which sport do you associate the terms <u>steeplechase</u> and <u>dressage</u>?

Who became president after Richard Nixon resigned?

Who wrote the sea classics <u>Moby Dick</u> and <u>Billy Budd</u>?

What is the largest living land animal?

How many days are in a leap year?

5, 136, 137, 138

In roman numerals, for what does the letter C stand?

CXIII

Which planet is the largest?

Was Sounder a hunting dog, a trumpet player, or a bull moose?

Which U.S. national park is the largest known area of underground chambers and passageways?

The narrator for the Sherlock Holmes mysteries is the detective's closest friend. What is his name?

Mowgli is the central character in what series of Kipling stories?

Who made the first solo nonstop flight across the Atlantic?

What do we call an unusually high sea wave caused by earth movement or volcanic eruption?

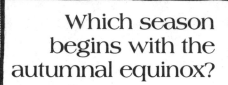

Which season begins with the autumnal equinox?

What is the largest living animal?

What is the earth's path around the sun called?

What man-made waterway connects the Atlantic and Pacific oceans?

Name the one-legged pirate in Stevenson's <u>Treasure Island</u>.

Name the first woman to be appointed to the U.S. Supreme Court.

What name is given to the tube that connects your throat to your stomach?

37

5
+3
8 ⟵

The result obtained when two or more numbers are added together is called what?

How many points does a football team receive for a field goal?

What do we call impressions, remnants, or traces of living things preserved in rocks?

For what does the abbreviation P.M. stand?

2:30 P.M.

In <u>Charlotte's Web</u>, what young girl prevents her father from killing the smallest pig in the litter?

On what city was the first atomic bomb dropped?

Name the woman who ran for vice-president of the United States on the Democratic ticket in 1984.

Where did the first airplane flight take place?

How many weeks are in a year?

What is a baby kangaroo called?

With which sport do you associate the terms <u>ball</u>, <u>mallet</u>, and <u>wicket</u>?

The result obtained when two or more numbers are multiplied is called what?

35×35=1225

Who wrote <u>Leaves of Grass</u>?

What was the name of the airplane in which Charles Lindbergh made his solo Atlantic crossing?

THREE MILE ISLAND

Do the words "Three Mile Island" name a Pacific island, a beach resort, or the site of a nuclear reactor?

What product did angry colonists dump into Boston Harbor?

The Question Collection
© 1988—The Learning Works, Inc.

In a poem by Eugene Field, which three characters sailed off in a wooden shoe?

Which rodent builds a dam?

What is the earth's only natural satellite?

There are how many centimeters in a meter?

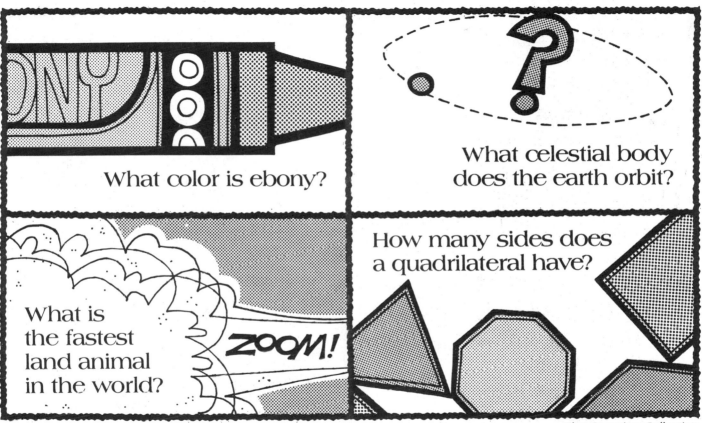

What color is ebony?

What celestial body does the earth orbit?

What is the fastest land animal in the world?

ZOOM!

How many sides does a quadrilateral have?

43

The Question Collection
© 1988—The Learning Works, Inc.

How many continents are there on the earth?

What was the name of Paul Bunyan's blue ox?

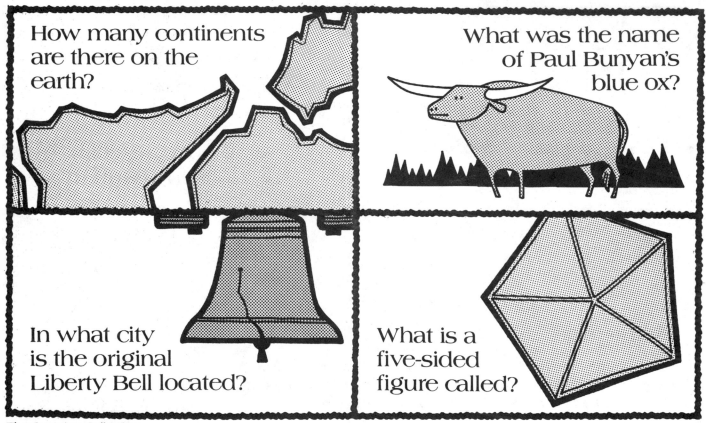

In what city is the original Liberty Bell located?

What is a five-sided figure called?

What cowboy-philosopher said, "I never met a man I didn't like"?

Which African mammals did Joy Adamson write about in <u>Born Free</u>?

Which desert is the world's largest?

Who was the leader of the Rough Riders?

45

What do we call the imaginary circle around the earth which lies halfway between the north and south poles?

Which ocean is the smallest?

What was Hans Brinker's prized possession?

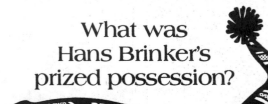

Name the two bicycle mechanics who built and flew the first successful airplane.

Water covers what fraction of the earth?

Who became president after John Kennedy was assassinated?

In Charlotte's Web, what is the name of the rat that lives under Wilbur's trough?

For whom was the state of Pennsylvania named?

How many years is one term of office for a U.S. president?

What is the title of Rudyard Kipling's book of animal stories in which he explains how the leopard got his spots?

What major U.S. city was destroyed by fire in 1906 after an earthquake had broken the water mains?

What was the name of Henry Ford's first mass-produced automobile?

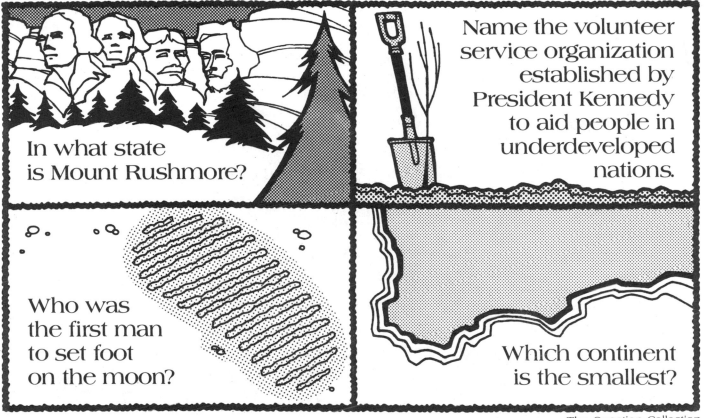

In what state is Mount Rushmore?

Name the volunteer service organization established by President Kennedy to aid people in underdeveloped nations.

Who was the first man to set foot on the moon?

Which continent is the smallest?

The Question Collection
© 1988–The Learning Works, Inc.

What is the normal body temperature for human beings?

What strong force pulls things toward the center of the earth?

What is a baby whale called?

What do we call the alternate rising and falling of the surface of the ocean which occurs twice a day?

What were the Communists operating in South Vietnam called?

Why do people see lightning before they hear thunder?

What is the distance around the outside edge of a circle called?

In Little Women, which one of the four sisters dies?

51

The Question Collection
© 1988—The Learning Works, Inc.

In what year was the Declaration of Independence signed?

What is the name of the grouchy, penny-pinching old man in Dickens's "A Christmas Carol"?

From what place in the United States are space vehicles launched?

Name the "unsinkable" British steamer that hit an iceberg and sank in the North Atlantic in 1912.

Name the Swiss family that is shipwrecked on a desert island and uses ingenuity to establish a European life-style there.

Which mineral is the hardest of all naturally occurring substances?

In what part of the human body is the "funny bone"?

How many oceans are there on the earth?

What is a line drawn from one side of a circle through the center to the other side of the circle called?

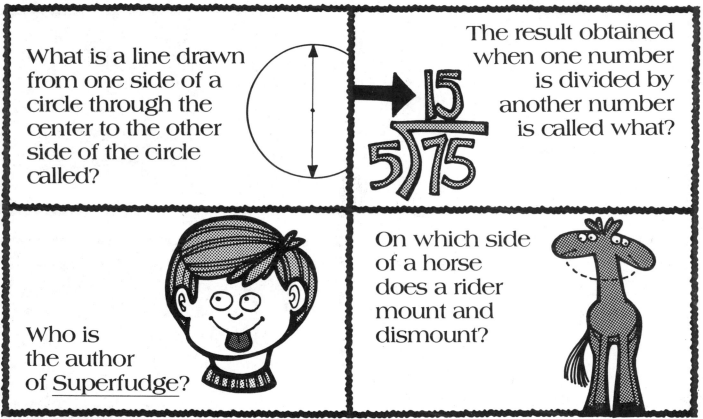

The result obtained when one number is divided by another number is called what?

Who is the author of Superfudge?

On which side of a horse does a rider mount and dismount?

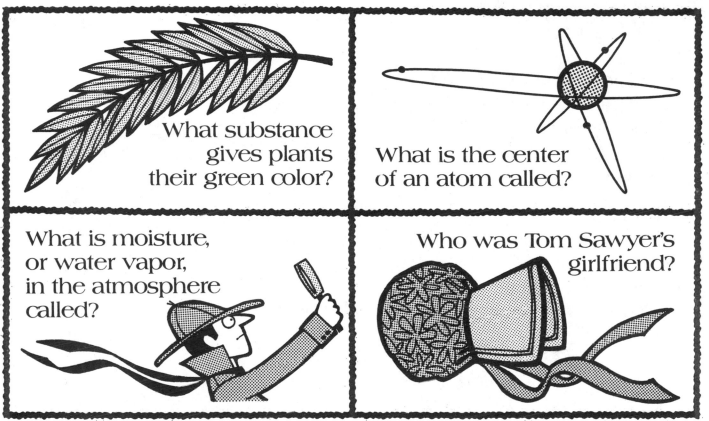

What substance gives plants their green color?

What is the center of an atom called?

What is moisture, or water vapor, in the atmosphere called?

Who was Tom Sawyer's girlfriend?

55

In which novel was the main character a one-eyed gun-fighting marshal named Rooster Cogburn?

What liquid metal is used in some thermometers?

Whose picture is on the dime?

I do solemnly swear that I will faithfully execute the office of President of the United States, and will, to the best of my ability, preserve, protect, and defend the Constitution of the United States.

At what ceremony does a U.S. president take the oath of office?

What important waterway was built to connect the Great Lakes with the Atlantic Ocean?

GREAT LAKES   ATLANTIC OCEAN

Which president designed, built, and lived in a home called Monticello?

E PLURIBUS UNUM
MONTICELLO
FIVE CENTS
ERICA

What is the highest court in the United States called?

What large black bird is the central figure in an alliterative poem by Edgar Allan Poe?

57

Who rode in the night to warn colonists that the British were coming?

Which continent is the largest?

How many sides does a hexagon have?

In Charlotte's Web, what does Fern name the runty pig she rescues?

Which is the largest country in South America?

For what does the abbreviation A.M. stand?

9:25 A.M.

Putt!

With which sport do you associate the terms bogey, driver, green, iron, putt, and wood?

75
-32
43

The result obtained when one number is subtracted from another number is called what?

Trees that do not shed their leaves in the fall are said to be what?

A sphinx has the body of what animal?

What do we call an angle that measures exactly 90 degrees?

90°

Who was the chaplain in Robin Hood's band?

Name the actor who became governor of California and then president of the United States.

In <u>Charlie and the Chocolate Factory</u>, who owned the chocolate factory?

What is the distance between the center and the edge of a circle called?

How many pints are in a gallon?

ONE GALLON
OIL BASE
ENAMEL PAINT
MIDNIGHT BLACK

The Question Collection
© 1988—The Learning Works, Inc.

I HAVE A DR

Who began a famous speech with the words, "I have a dream"?

Who was the first woman to make a transoceanic flight?

Who was the youngest sister in Little Women?

Washington, D.C. 20037

What do the letters D.C. stand for in the name Washington, D.C.?

Where did Abraham Lincoln give the speech that begins with the words "Four score and seven years ago"?

Name the imaginary country in Gulliver's Travels where people are so small that an ordinary man becomes a giant.

RE-ELECT PRESIDENT ROBINSON!

How many terms can a U.S. president serve?

What name was given to Great Plains farmlands stripped of topsoil by drought and wind?

The Question Collection
© 1988--The Learning Works, Inc.

What are the
three states
of matter?

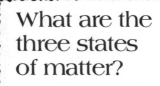

What are the names
of the two major
political parties
in the United States?

The War of 1812
was fought against
what country?

Name the profiteer
who becomes
Scarlet O'Hara's
third husband
in Gone With
the Wind.

What instrument is used to measure air pressure?

Who shot President John F. Kennedy?

What is the largest land bird in North America?

What do we call the study of celestial bodies and of their magnitudes, motions, and constitutions?

65

In what city is NASA Mission Control for space vehicles located?

What did kids have to find to be allowed inside Willy Wonka's chocolate factory?

How many years are in a decade?

During World War II, who was prime minister of Great Britain?

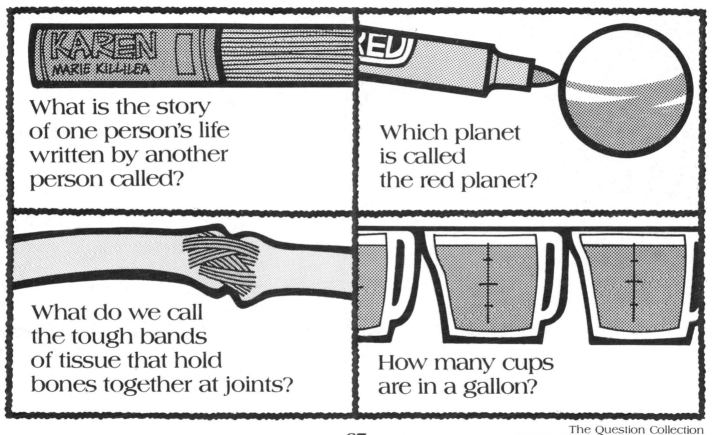

What is the story
of one person's life
written by another
person called?

Which planet
is called
the red planet?

What do we call
the tough bands
of tissue that hold
bones together at joints?

How many cups
are in a gallon?

67

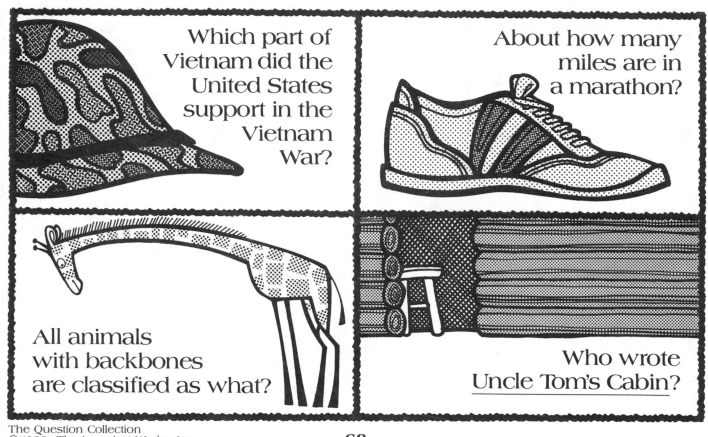

Which part of Vietnam did the United States support in the Vietnam War?

About how many miles are in a marathon?

All animals with backbones are classified as what?

Who wrote Uncle Tom's Cabin?

What do we call a narrow strip of land that separates two bodies of water and connects two larger areas of land?

Which one of the sisters in Little Women liked to write?

Which American statesman and scientist invented the bifocal lens?

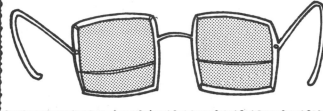

Who was the youngest man ever to serve as president of the United States?

How many degrees are in a circle?

What is the art of Japanese paper folding called?

What do we call a natural or man-made body that revolves around a planet?

What kind of stories did Aesop write?

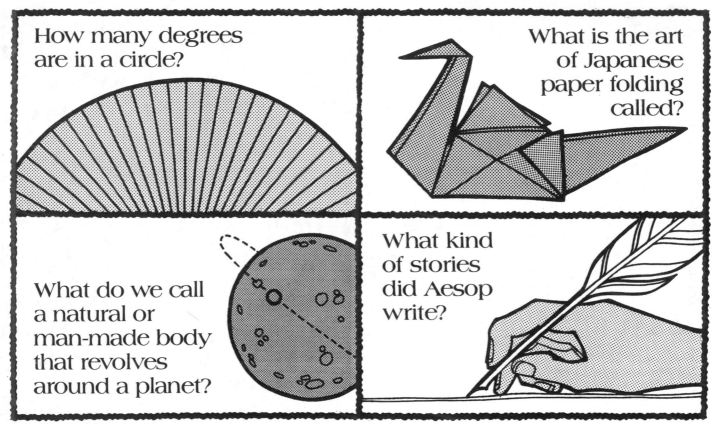

In which month does summer officially begin?

Which two animals fought a duel in a poem by Eugene Field?

Which planet in our solar system has the most moons?

Which is the largest living reptile?

71

What was President Lincoln's document freeing the slaves called?

Which vitamin is called the "sunshine vitamin"?

Which part of speech tells how, when, or where about a verb, an adjective, or an adverb?

Who wrote The Trumpet of the Swan?

Who invented the cotton gin?

What do we call an angle that measures less than 90 degrees?

Who said, "Speak softly and carry a big stick"?

What is the motto of the United States of America?

73

In *Where the Red Fern Grows*, were Old Dan and Little Ann mules, coonhounds, or people?

Name the highest mountain in the world.

Who was the oldest man to be elected president of the United States?

Who invented the magnetic telegraph?

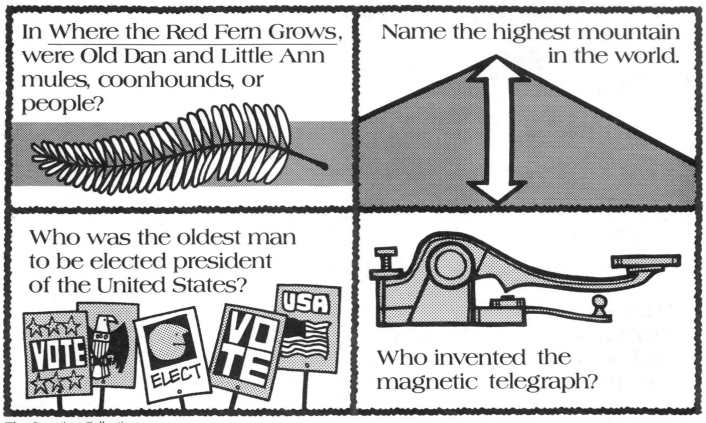

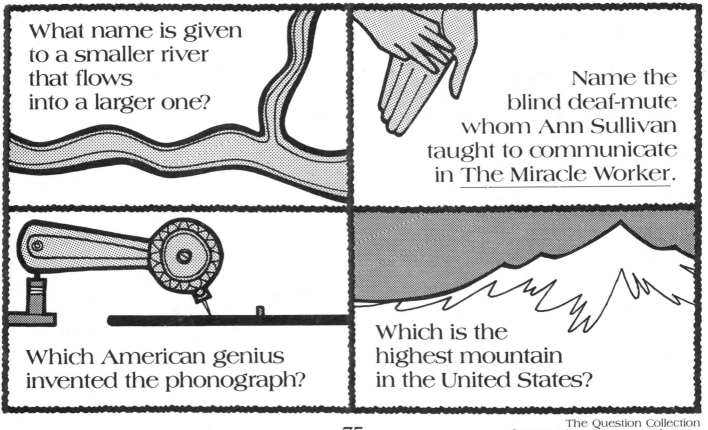

What name is given to a smaller river that flows into a larger one?

Name the blind deaf-mute whom Ann Sullivan taught to communicate in The Miracle Worker.

Which American genius invented the phonograph?

Which is the highest mountain in the United States?

In Henry Wadsworth Longfellow's poem, who stood under the spreading chestnut tree?

What name is given to an imaginary semicircle on the earth which reaches from pole to pole?

Which U.S. national park is home to a geyser named Old Faithful?

In which country would you find the second highest mountain in the world?

At what temperature does water boil?

What is the "lead" in a pencil really made of?

From whom were Anne Frank and her family hiding?

Who said, "That's one small step for a man, one giant leap for mankind"?

77

Who was the first vice-president of the United States of America?

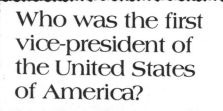

Which famous artist painted the ceiling of the Sistine Chapel?

Where were the first modern Olympic Games held?

Which author wrote more than 156 fairy tales, including "The Ugly Duckling" and "The Emperor's New Clothes"?

Which state is the setting for The Call of the Wild?

In what building was Abraham Lincoln shot?

In 1803 the United States purchased the Louisiana Territory for $15 million from what country?

Margaret Mitchell wrote only one novel. What was it?

79

In humans, which teeth are the last to come in?

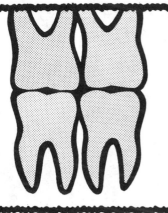

What were American foot soldiers called during World War I?

Name the runaway slave who is Huckleberry Finn's companion on a raft trip down the Mississippi.

♥ FEBRUARY ♥

1	2	3	4	5	6	7	8	9	10	11	12	13	14
15	16	17	18	19	20	21	22	23	24	25	26	27	28
29													

How often does a leap year occur?

What is the hardest substance in the human body?

Who said, "Give me liberty or give me death"?

Where was the Headless Horseman often seen?

How long does it take for the earth to complete one orbit around the sun?

81

On what island does the Statue of Liberty stand?

In which novel did John Steinbeck describe the plight of the Okies?

What European country financed Columbus's 1492 expedition?

In what part of the human body would you find an iris?

Where did the rails of the Central Pacific and Union Pacific railroads meet?

Busts of which four U.S. presidents are carved on the face of Mount Rushmore?

Androcles extracted a thorn from the paw of what kind of animal?

Which American city did Carl Sandburg call "Hog Butcher for the World"?

Name the Boston structure in which signal lights were placed to indicate whether the British were coming by land or by sea.

The stock market crash of 1929 led to what historical era?

Name the three branches of the federal government.

Which H. G. Wells science fiction novel recounts the adventures of a time traveler?

Who wrote
Charlotte's Web?

What do we call the
direct exchange of
goods for goods or
goods for services
without the use
of money?

What were
Franklin Roosevelt's
radio talks to the
American people called?

Which country
is the largest
in the world?

85

In roman numerals, for what does the letter M stand?

The process of periodically moving from one climatic region to another to feed or breed is called what?

What scale is used to measure the intensity of earthquakes?

In which Missouri town was the book The Adventures of Tom Sawyer set?

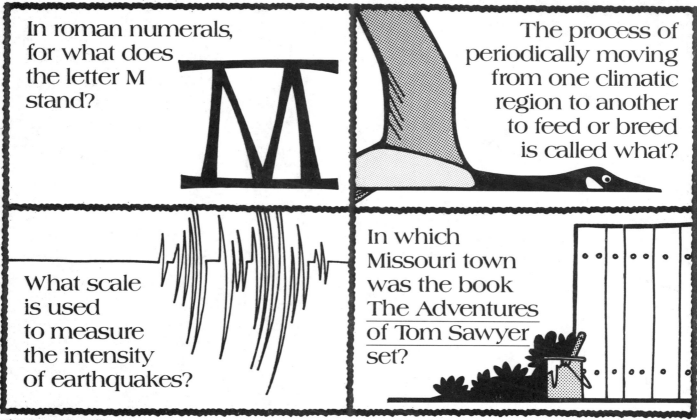

How many senators does each state send to the U.S. Congress?

Which planet is farthest from the sun?

During the American Revolution, where was George Washington's winter headquarters?

Which Shakespearean play is about two star-crossed lovers who are overwhelmed by the problems they must face?

By means of a potion, Dr. Jekyll changed himself into a brutal man known by what name?

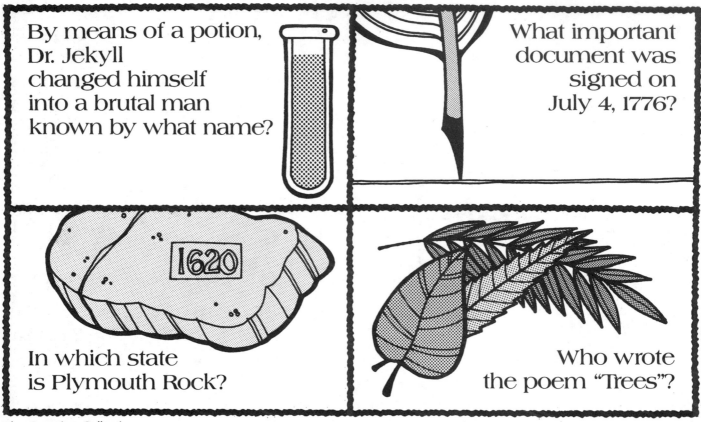

What important document was signed on July 4, 1776?

In which state is Plymouth Rock?

Who wrote the poem "Trees"?

Which novel chronicles Captain Ahab's search for a great white whale?

Who was the first president to live in the White House?

What name is given to the place where a river begins?

Which famous American statesman published Poor Richard's Almanack?

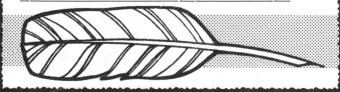

89

What are the dark patches on the surface of the sun called?

What general commanded the Confederate forces during the Civil War?

In which month does winter officially begin?

At what temperature does water freeze?

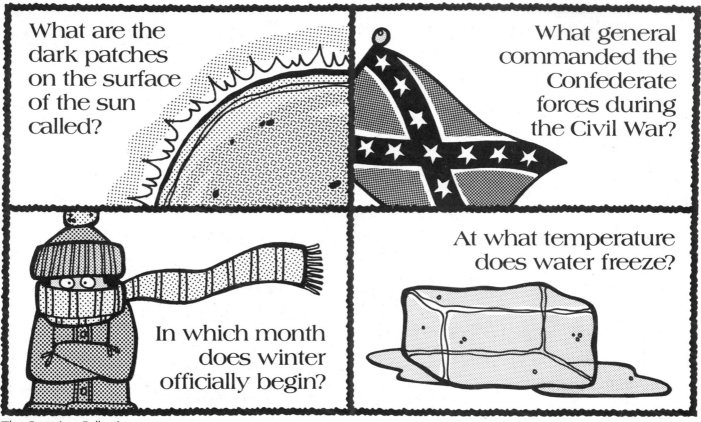

Which Great Lake lies entirely within the boundaries of the United States?

What part of speech tells which one, what kind, or how many about a noun or pronoun?

How often is the U.S. census taken?

Name the army scout who toured the world with his Wild West Show.

91

Which planet is nearest to the earth?

Name the story by Mark Twain in which a street beggar exchanges places with a prince.

How many players are on an ice hockey team?

Who was elected president of the Confederacy?

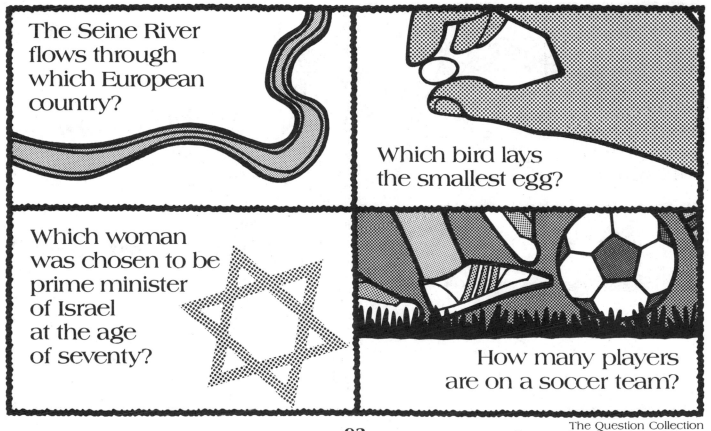

The Seine River flows through which European country?

Which bird lays the smallest egg?

Which woman was chosen to be prime minister of Israel at the age of seventy?

How many players are on a soccer team?

The Question Collection
© 1988—The Learning Works, Inc.

Who was America's first man in space?

What nickname did Andrew Jackson's troops give him?

During World War II, where did Japan first attack the United States?

Name the famous English detective created by A. Conan Doyle.

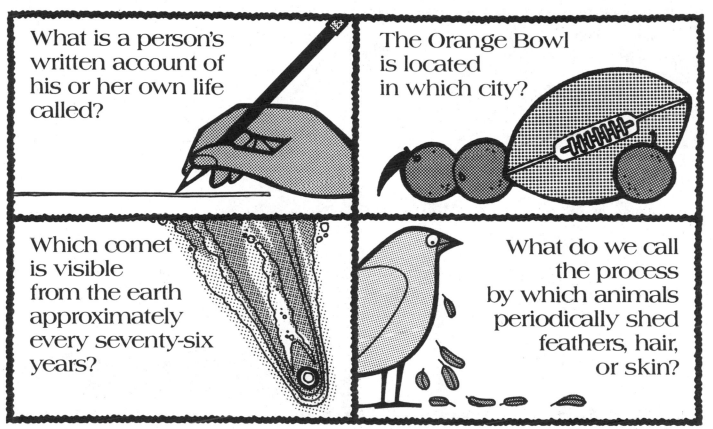

What is a person's written account of his or her own life called?

The Orange Bowl is located in which city?

Which comet is visible from the earth approximately every seventy-six years?

What do we call the process by which animals periodically shed feathers, hair, or skin?

95

Name the five Great Lakes.

Name the adventure story in which six men set out to sail a balsa-wood raft from South America to Polynesia.

In the poem by Coleridge, what was the Ancient Mariner doomed to wear around his neck?

What Indian woman acted as a guide for Lewis and Clark when they explored the Louisiana Purchase?

How long does the moon take to orbit the earth?

Who wrote Little Women?

Stories that recount facts are classified as what?

What was George Washington's wife's name?

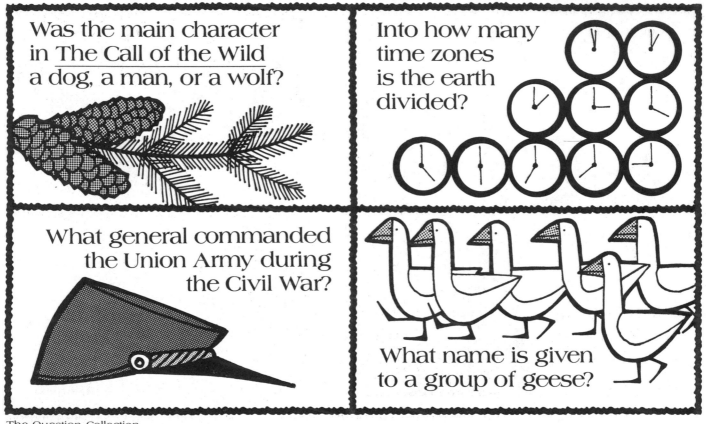

Was the main character in The Call of the Wild a dog, a man, or a wolf?

Into how many time zones is the earth divided?

What general commanded the Union Army during the Civil War?

What name is given to a group of geese?

Which English navigator discovered the Hudson River?

In what city was the U.S. Constitution written?

What illustrator painted American life covers for the <u>Saturday Evening Post</u> from 1916 until 1963?

In what novel is Jody Baxter's pet fawn shot by his mother because it eats the plants in her garden?

What do we call an imaginary circle on the earth that runs parallel to the equator?

Name the sequel to <u>Little Women</u>, which is set in a boys' school run by Jo and her husband.

Who wrote "The Star Spangled Banner"?

In which U.S. national park would you find the world's tallest living things?

Who wrote stories about a boy named Christopher Robin and a bear named Winnie-the-Pooh?

Name the artist who painted the <u>Mona Lisa</u>.

Name the U.S. swimmer who won seven gold medals in the 1972 Olympic Games.

Which planet is nearest to the sun?

The Question Collection
© 1988—The Learning Works, Inc.

What is the fastest flying animal?

What fighting group became famous during the Spanish-American War by winning the battle of San Juan Hill?

Name the Indian lad who played "by the shores of Gitche Gumee."

Which season begins with the vernal equinox?

Where and when was John F. Kennedy assassinated?

What was the fast overland mail service between Missouri and California called?

Trees that shed their leaves every fall are said to be what?

In what novel does a black man help a group of nuns build a church?

103

What name is given to the painting technique in which a picture is created by applying small dots of color to a surface?

Which European country is the setting for John Hersey's A Bell for Adano?

What international organization was formed after World War I to prevent future wars?

What is the name of the San Francisco Giants' home stadium?

Which fruit is sometimes called an alligator pear?

In To Kill a Mockingbird, what is the profession of Atticus Finch?

Name the mission where a small band of Texans made a stand against the Mexican army and were all killed.

What do we call a scientist who studies fossil remains to learn about past geologic periods?

What nonfiction book
by Rachel Carson
led to the banning
of the chemical DDT?

ck tock tick tock

Name the device
that marks time
for musicians.

Which planet is between
the earth and Jupiter?

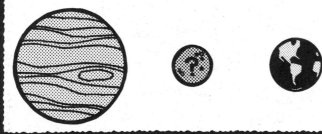

Who commanded the
Continental Army
during the American
Revolution?

Who was the first man in space?

Who was president of the United States at the start of the Great Depression?

In one of John Steinbeck's novels, what valuable jewel brings bad luck to an Indian family?

How many zeros are in one billion?

107

When, in the course of human events, it becomes necessary for one people to dissolve the political bands which have connected them with another...

In what building is the Declaration of Independence kept?

When asked to surrender, what American naval hero replied, "Sir, I have not yet begun to fight"?

Northerners who came to the South after the Civil War seeking private gain under the reconstruction governments were called what?

South

How many keys are on a piano?

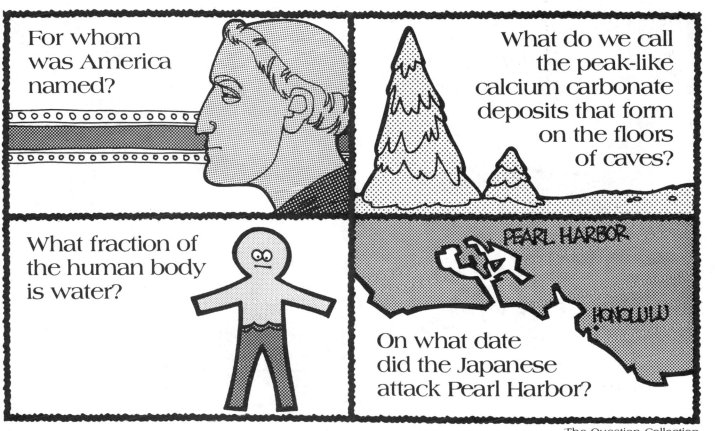

For whom was America named?

What do we call the peak-like calcium carbonate deposits that form on the floors of caves?

What fraction of the human body is water?

On what date did the Japanese attack Pearl Harbor?

PEARL HARBOR

109

In 1987, a painting entitled Sunflowers sold for more than $39 million. Who painted Sunflowers?

For what purpose is Buck used in Jack London's story The Call of the Wild?

VICTORY! VICTORY! VICTORY! VICTORY! VICTORY!

Which U.S. president was elected to four consecutive terms?

Who designed, built, and flew an enormous wooden airplane called the Spruce Goose?

Name the female prohibitionist who broke up saloons with a hatchet.

In the Oklahoma run, people who settled on land before it was officially opened were called what?

Who wrote Around the World in Eighty Days?

During World War II, America's friends were called the Allied powers. What name was given to enemy nations?

The Question Collection
© 1988—The Learning Works, Inc.

What black leader led the bus boycott in Montgomery, Alabama?

Which planet is sometimes called the morning star or the evening star?

The practice of making political appointments in return for political party service is called what?

Who compiled the first American Dictionary of the English language?

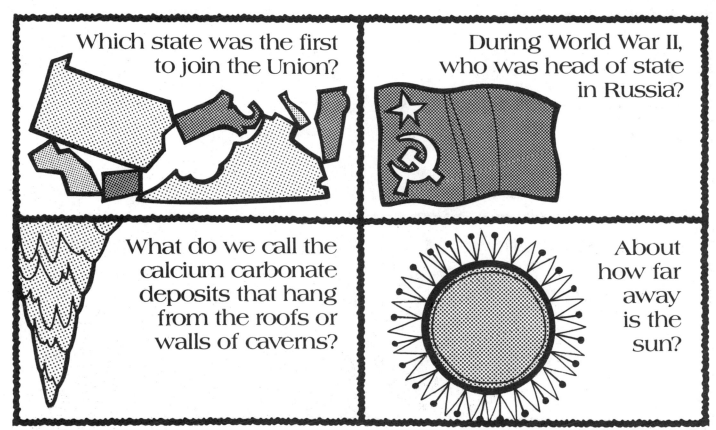

Which state was the first to join the Union?

During World War II, who was head of state in Russia?

What do we call the calcium carbonate deposits that hang from the roofs or walls of caverns?

About how far away is the sun?

113

In roman numerals, for what does the letter L stand?

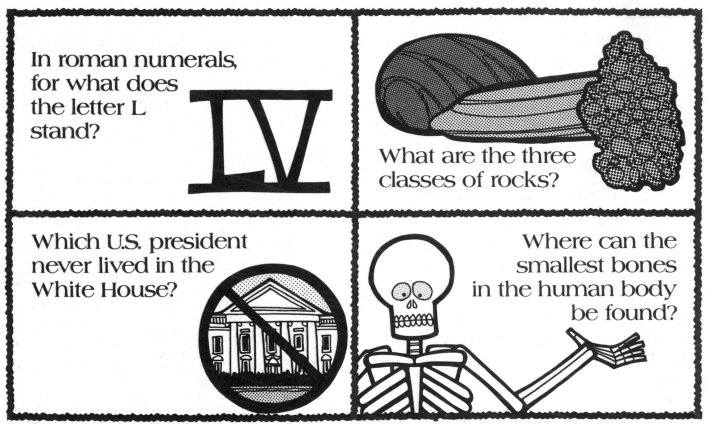

What are the three classes of rocks?

Which U.S. president never lived in the White House?

Where can the smallest bones in the human body be found?

In which galaxy is the planet earth?

Name the young Frenchman who became a major general in the Continental Army.

Who was the sole surviving member of Anne Frank's family?

Which bone is the longest and strongest in the human skeleton?

What name was given to the policy statement by President James Monroe warning European nations not to interfere in the Western Hemisphere?

James Monroe

In what area is <u>Roll of Thunder Hear My Cry</u> set?

What do we call an angle that measures more than 90 degrees but less than 180 degrees?

By what other name are weather forecasters known?

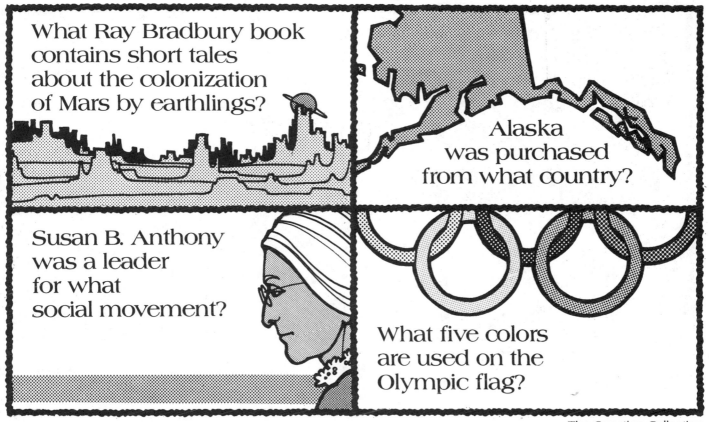

What Ray Bradbury book contains short tales about the colonization of Mars by earthlings?

Alaska was purchased from what country?

Susan B. Anthony was a leader for what social movement?

What five colors are used on the Olympic flag?

117

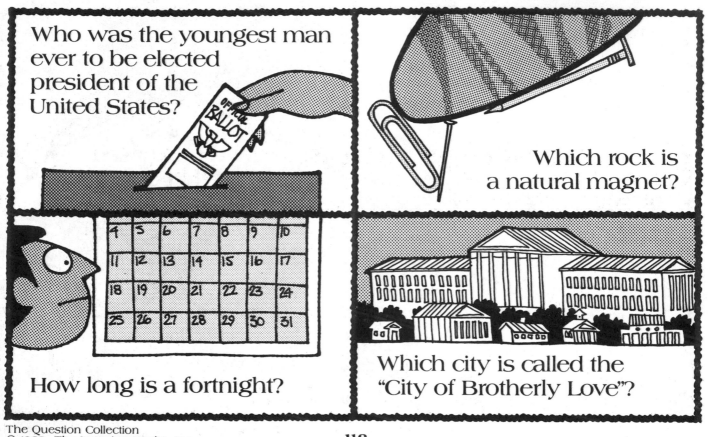

Who was the youngest man ever to be elected president of the United States?

Which rock is a natural magnet?

How long is a fortnight?

Which city is called the "City of Brotherly Love"?

The Scopes trial in Tennessee dealt with the teaching of what scientific theory?

FOUNDED · 1565

What is the oldest city in the United States?

What building is the tallest in the world?

Who gives Huckleberry Finn a home and tries to civilize him?

The Question Collection
© 1988—The Learning Works, Inc.

Name the two men who were commissioned by President Jefferson to explore the vast Louisiana Purchase.

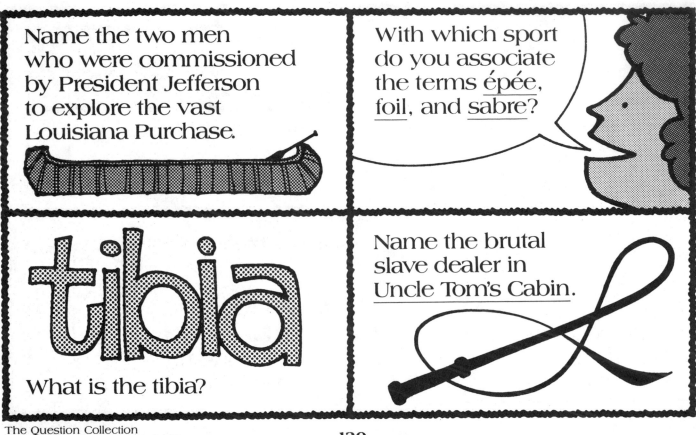

With which sport do you associate the terms épée, foil, and sabre?

What is the tibia?

Name the brutal slave dealer in Uncle Tom's Cabin.

Which officer in the Continental Army plotted to surrender West Point to the British and became known as a traitor?

Name the trophy that is awarded annually to the champion team in the National Hockey League.

Which national park contains the highest peak in the contiguous United States?

In <u>The Trumpet of the Swan</u>, what is wrong with Louis?

Which colonial city became known for its witchcraft trials?

What is the popular name for frozen carbon dioxide?

How many feet are in a mile?

336,337,338

What well-known poem by Rudyard Kipling has a two-letter word for its title?

Which nineteenth-century French artist frequently used ballet dancers as the subjects of his paintings?

Which Spanish explorer landed in Florida on May 30, 1539?

What was Franklin Roosevelt's program for economic reform called?

Who was the youngest tennis player ever to compete at Wimbledon?

The Question Collection
© 1988—The Learning Works, Inc.

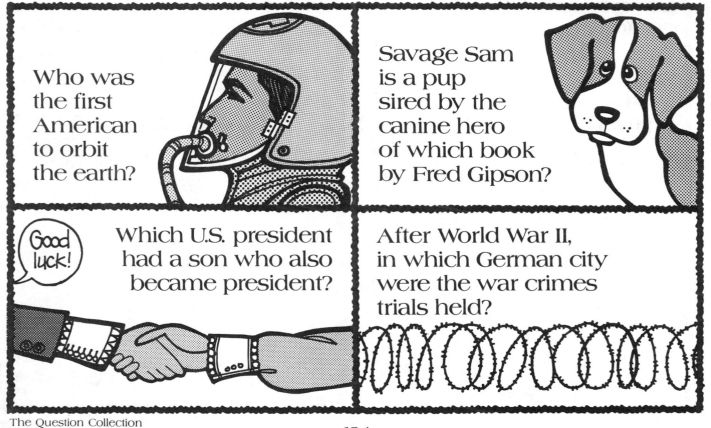

Who was the first American to orbit the earth?

Savage Sam is a pup sired by the canine hero of which book by Fred Gipson?

Good luck!

Which U.S. president had a son who also became president?

After World War II, in which German city were the war crimes trials held?

Who was president of the United States during World War I?

Which planet is the smallest?

Which artist created the "decorations" for the first edition of Winnie-the-Pooh?

Under what name did Samuel Langhorne Clemens write?

The Question Collection
© 1988—The Learning Works, Inc.

Which Steinbeck novel describes a migrant farm worker's attempt to look after his strong but simple-minded friend?

Bruce Jenner, Rafer Johnson, Robert Mathias, and Bill Toomey are all winners of which Olympic event?

mandolin

What is a mandolin?

What was the Allied invasion of the European continent through Normandy called?

What is the first layer of the earth's atmosphere called?

What is a karat used to measure?

How many chambers does the human heart have?

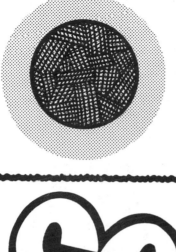

In what war did Spain give up claim to Cuba, Puerto Rico, Guam, and the Philippines?

Remember the Maine!

127

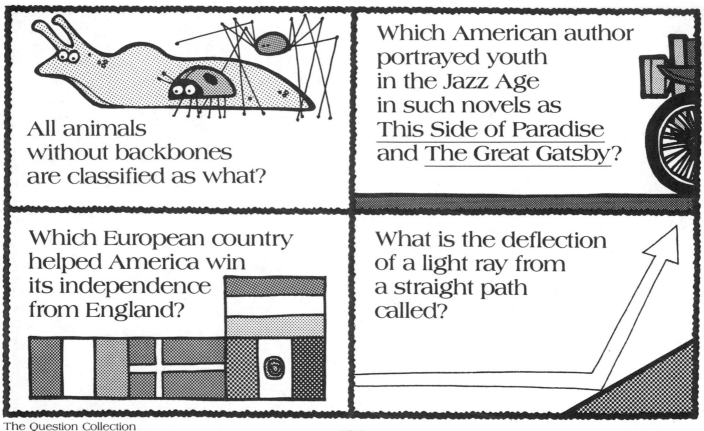

All animals
without backbones
are classified as what?

Which American author
portrayed youth
in the Jazz Age
in such novels as
<u>This Side of Paradise</u>
and <u>The Great Gatsby</u>?

Which European country
helped America win
its independence
from England?

What is the deflection
of a light ray from
a straight path
called?

With which sport do you associate the terms <u>chipping</u>, <u>dribbling</u>, <u>heading</u>, and <u>volleying</u>?

Who drafted the Declaration of Independence?

Who painted the picture of a Midwestern farm couple entitled <u>American Gothic</u>?

What is the top layer of the earth called?

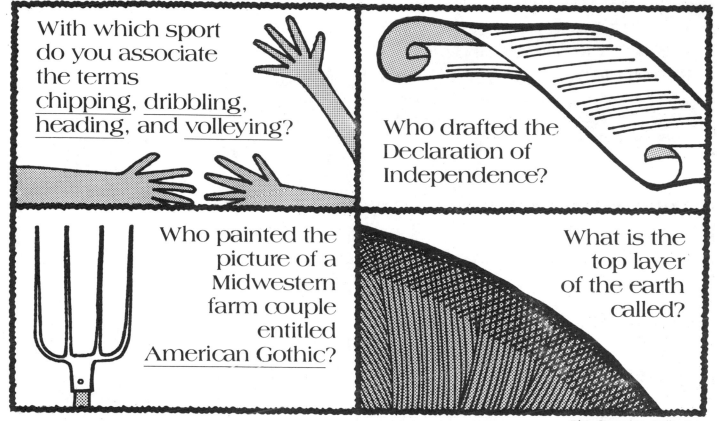

129

Which country is the second largest in the world?

Who was in charge of the Jamestown English colony?

By what other name is a <u>mapmaker</u> known?

What was Clement Moore's poem "'Twas the Night Before Christmas" originally called?

What does a numismatist collect?

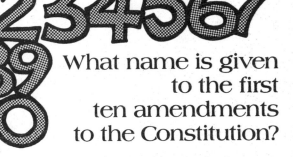

What name is given to the first ten amendments to the Constitution?

In what short story was a naval officer exiled at sea and not permitted to hear the name of his native country?

What do we call a scientist who studies the material remains of past human life and activities?

Name the elderly slave who told stories about the escapades of Brer Rabbit.

How many points does a football team receive for a safety?

Scientists who study animals and their classifications are called what?

Where did General Robert E. Lee surrender, ending the Civil War?

What current novel is about a Cro-Magnon girl who is adopted by Neanderthals?

shall not be denied or

What right did the 19th Amendment to the U.S. Constitution guarantee to women?

Where is the Tomb of the Unknown Soldier?

What is the largest bird in the world?

What part
of a flower
holds the pollen?

Roderick Usher
is the main character
in what story
by Edgar Allan Poe?

What was the site
of the first
English colony
in the New World,
which later became known
as the "lost colony"?

What is the
outer layer
of a person's
skin called?

Name the former slave who established Tuskegee Institute for the education of freed slaves.

Name the gawky schoolmaster in Washington Irving's "Legend of Sleepy Hollow."

What does a philatelist collect?

MY COLLECTION

Name the trail over which wagon trains carried settlers to the Pacific Northwest.

135

The Question Collection
© 1988—The Learning Works, Inc.

How many years are in a score?

Name the famous trail over which cattle were driven north from Texas to railheads in Abilene, Kansas.

What set of debates swept Abraham Lincoln to national prominence even though he lost his bid for a seat in the U.S. Senate?

★ ABE THE GIANT KILLER! ★

Name the girl Ichabod Crane courts in "The Legend of Sleepy Hollow."

Name the Kipling novel in which a wealthy American boy is washed overboard enroute to Europe and is picked up by a fishing schooner.

How many bones are in the adult human body?

Which planet is the fastest?

Name the Shawnee Indian chief who fought on the British side during the War of 1812 and was killed.

Name the Dutch mathematician and physicist who invented the pendulum clock.

In which county did Mark Twain's celebrated frog jump?

Name the thirteen-year-old girl who is the main character in Homecoming.

Which U.S. national park contains two active volcanoes?

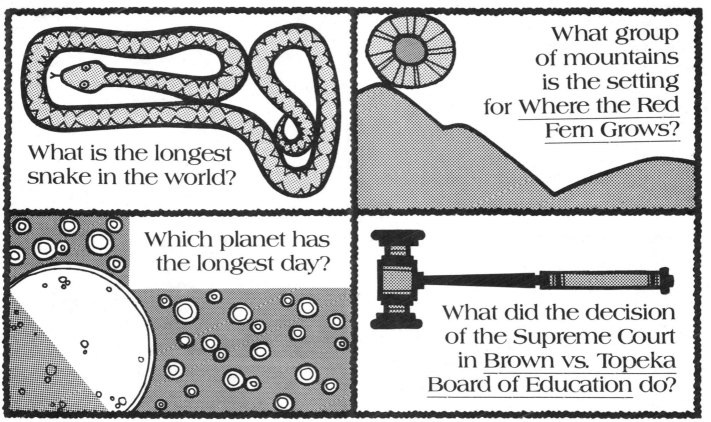

What is the longest snake in the world?

What group of mountains is the setting for Where the Red Fern Grows?

Which planet has the longest day?

What did the decision of the Supreme Court in Brown vs. Topeka Board of Education do?

What name is given to the layer of the earth which lies just beneath the crust?

Which U.S. president was known as the "Father of the Constitution"?

What is the name of the simple-minded giant in Steinbeck's Of Mice and Men?

How many rings does Saturn have?

In North America, what is the shortest day of the year?

Which sea is the saltiest in the world?

Which element makes up about 80 percent of dry air?

At the close of the American Revolution, where did the surrounded British forces surrender?

The Question Collection
© 1988—The Learning Works, Inc.

Who led the expedition that first opened diplomatic and trade relations between the United States and Japan?

How much does the shot used in Olympic shot put competition weigh?

Which bird can fly backward?

In <u>Moby Dick</u>, with what does Captain Ahab replace his missing leg?

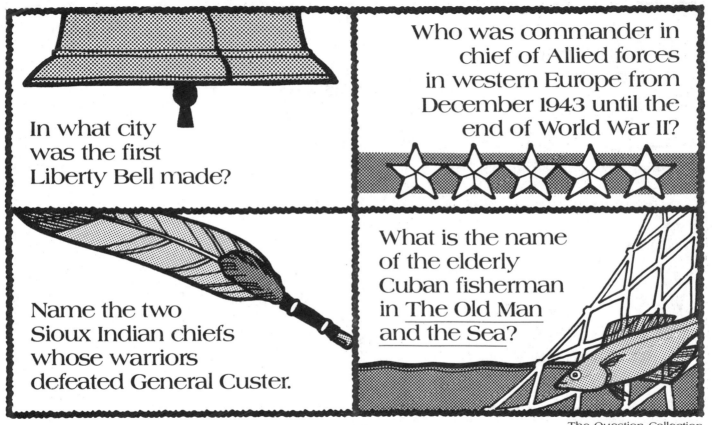

In what city was the first Liberty Bell made?

Who was commander in chief of Allied forces in western Europe from December 1943 until the end of World War II?

Name the two Sioux Indian chiefs whose warriors defeated General Custer.

What is the name of the elderly Cuban fisherman in The Old Man and the Sea?

What was the name of Robert Fulton's steamboat?

What other name is given to the pole star or north star?

Which illustrator was commissioned to create pictures for the revised edition of the Laura Ingalls Wilder books, first published in 1953?

Who led an unsuccessful Negro slave revolt in 1831?

Which U.S. city was the site of the first United Nations meeting?

PHILADELPHIA
SAN FRANCISCO
NEW YORK
LOS ANGELES

Name the Indian chief who befriended the Jamestown colonists.

When and where were the words for "The Star-Spangled Banner" written?

In which Lois Duncan book did Laurie look into a mirror and see her reflection smile when she had not?

The Question Collection
© 1988—The Learning Works, Inc.

Where would you find the world's oldest living tree?

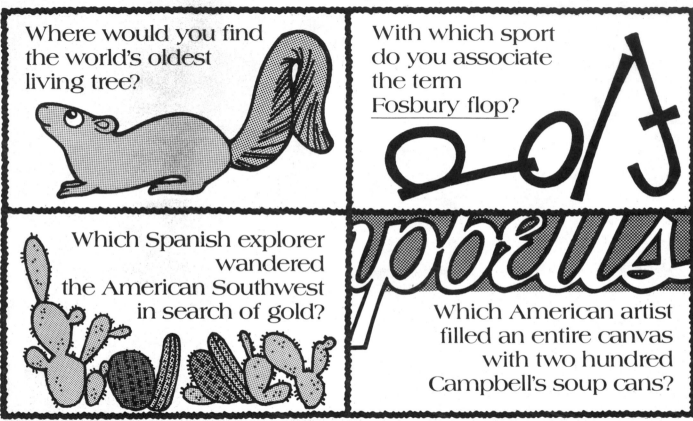

With which sport do you associate the term <u>Fosbury flop</u>?

Which Spanish explorer wandered the American Southwest in search of gold?

Which American artist filled an entire canvas with two hundred Campbell's soup cans?

What slogan was used
in the election campaign
of William Henry Harrison?

What was
Hiawatha's
wife's name?

Name the book
by Robert Cormier
which was inspired
by his son's reluctance
to sell chocolate
for his school.

Which French explorer
sailed up the
St. Lawrence River
to the Lachine Rapids
in 1603?

Which English philanthropist founded the colony of Georgia?

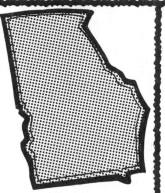

Which American woman artist lived in New Mexico for many years and is known for her paintings of plants, cattle skulls, and uncluttered desert scenes?

What U.S. woman won gold medals in the eighty-meter hurdles and the javelin throw at the 1932 Olympics?

With whom does Anna Karénina fall in love?

Who was president of the U. S. when the Panama Canal was constructed?

Which American artist is perhaps best known for a picture he painted of his mother seated in a chair?

Excluding the sun, which star in our galaxy is nearest to the earth?

In a short story by Bret Harte, what western community decides to rid itself of improper persons?

Name the son of Chingachgook in The Last of the Mohicans.

In 1987, a painting entitled Irises sold for $53.9 million. Who painted Irises?

Where is the annual All-American Soap Box Derby held?

OUT IN

Which president was impeached by the House of Representatives and then acquitted?

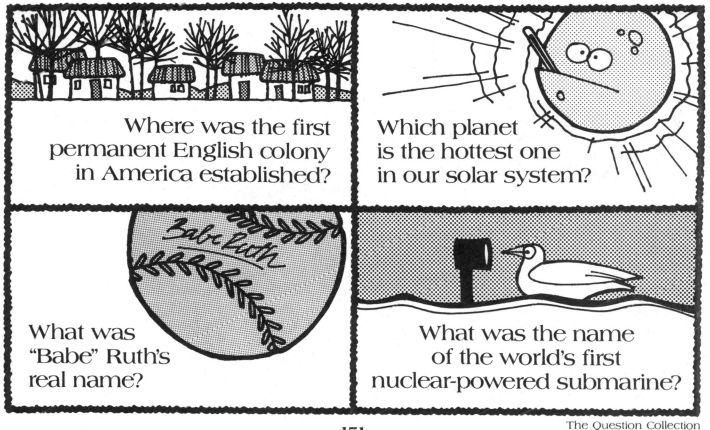

Where was the first permanent English colony in America established?

Which planet is the hottest one in our solar system?

What was "Babe" Ruth's real name?

What was the name of the world's first nuclear-powered submarine?

The Question Collection
© 1988—The Learning Works, Inc.

During World War II, who was prime minister of Japan?

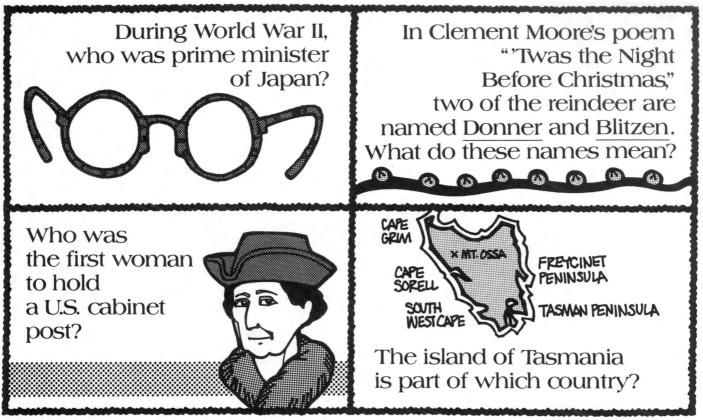

In Clement Moore's poem "'Twas the Night Before Christmas," two of the reindeer are named Donner and Blitzen. What do these names mean?

Who was the first woman to hold a U.S. cabinet post?

CAPE GRIM

X MT. OSSA

CAPE SORELL

FREYCINET PENINSULA

SOUTH WEST CAPE

TASMAN PENINSULA

The island of Tasmania is part of which country?

Which national park is the largest remaining subtropical wilderness in the continental United States?

In When the Legends Die, Thomas Black Bull is injured in what kind of accident?

What name is given to the longitude line that is labeled 0° and passes through Greenwich, England?

◆ **Greenwich**

Which Swedish manufacturer invented dynamite?

BAM!

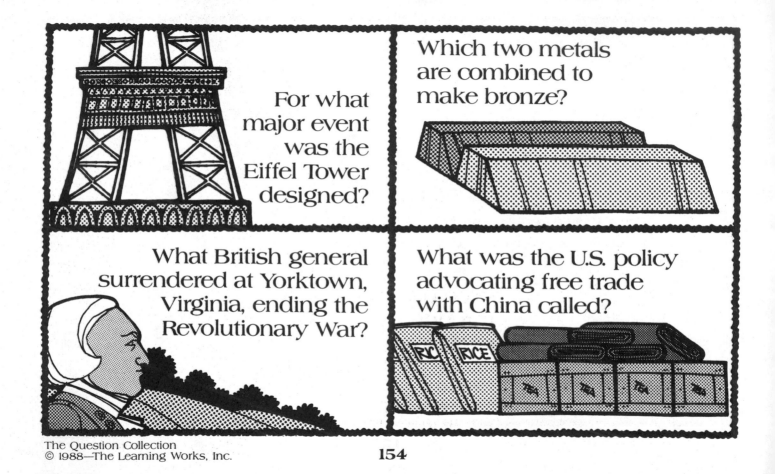

For what major event was the Eiffel Tower designed?

Which two metals are combined to make bronze?

What British general surrendered at Yorktown, Virginia, ending the Revolutionary War?

What was the U.S. policy advocating free trade with China called?

RICE

Who was the first governor of Massachusetts Bay Colony?

Who commanded the American forces in France during World War I?

Name the world's largest inland waterway.

Lewis Carroll is the pseudonym of the man who wrote Alice's Adventures in Wonderland. What is this man's real name?

What was the popular name of the frigate U.S.S. Constitution?

After American soldiers had surrendered in the Philippines, they were forced to march to the Japanese prison camps. What is this march called?

In what novel did lonely people talk to a deaf-mute who could not hear them?

Name the Cherokee Indian who developed an alphabet for his people.

The Question Collection
© 1988—The Learning Works, Inc.

Who was the first chief justice of the U.S. Supreme Court?

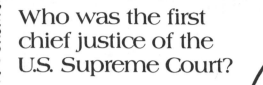

What was the name of the British warship on which Billy Budd served?

In Longfellow's narrative poem <u>The Courtship of Miles Standish</u>, who tells John Alden to speak for himself?

Who was the most famous Nez Percé Indian chief?

What was the name of the horse Ichabod Crane rode in "The Legend of Sleepy Hollow"?

What is the second layer of the earth's atmosphere called?

What is the largest living primate?

What nickname was given to Baron Manfred von Richthofen, the German flying ace of World War I?

Who was the scout for John C. Frémont's exploration of the Rocky Mountains?

Which American family has produced three generations of successful artists named Newell, Andrew, and Jamie?

What do bowlers call three strikes in a row?

1737·1809

Who wrote the pamphlet Common Sense?

By what other name is the European Recovery Program known?

Which U.S. president had the shortest term of office?

Name the Puritan captain in Longfellow's poem who was too shy to propose to his girlfriend.

Where was the first shot of the Civil War fired?

Who wrote
the narrative poem
<u>Evangeline</u>?

Name the battle
in which U.S. troops
massacred two hundred
Sioux Indians.

Name the first black
to be appointed to the
U.S. Supreme Court.

In North America,
what is the longest
day of the year?

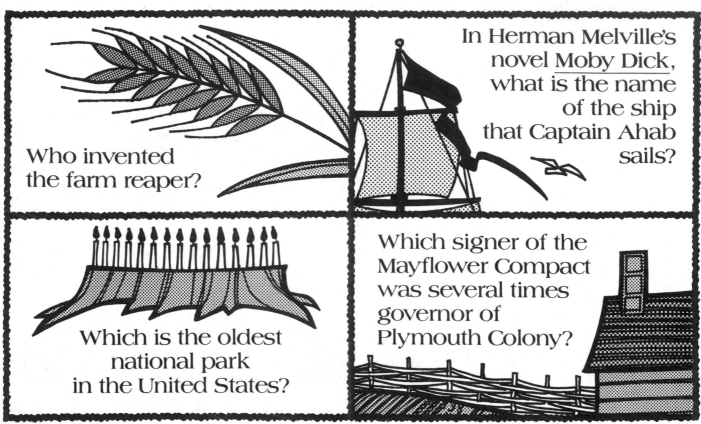

Who invented the farm reaper?

In Herman Melville's novel <u>Moby Dick</u>, what is the name of the ship that Captain Ahab sails?

Which is the oldest national park in the United States?

Which signer of the Mayflower Compact was several times governor of Plymouth Colony?

In which U.S. national park would you find the nation's highest waterfall?

What was the name of America's first satellite?

Name the London street beggar who exchanges places with the Prince of Wales in a historical romance written by Mark Twain.

Name the place in California where gold was first discovered.

The Question Collection
© 1988—The Learning Works, Inc.

In <u>East of Eden</u>, which Trask twin joins the army and is killed?

Which U.S. president served two nonconsecutive terms in that office?

1885·1889 1893·1897

How long was the first flight by the Wright brothers?

Who wrote the Pledge of Allegiance to the Flag?

How old was S. E. Hinton when her book The Outsiders was published?

The sinking of what battleship in the Caribbean influenced the United States to declare war on Spain?

Who invented the sewing machine?

What was Willie Mays's uniform number when he played with the Giants?

165

The Question Collection
© 1988—The Learning Works, Inc.

What was Hoover Dam originally called?

What American general defeated the British at the battle of New Orleans?

Who killed Alexander Hamilton in a pistol duel?

Which state is called the "mother of presidents" because eight U.S. chief executives were born there?

The Five Civilized Tribes were forcibly moved to what is now Oklahoma. What was their tragic journey called?

Who was the first American author to be awarded the Nobel Prize for literature?

Who was the first black to play baseball in the major leagues?

Name the first mass-produced computer.

167

Who was the first woman to swim across the English Channel?

Where was the first capitol of the United States of America?

The humorous World War II satire Mister Roberts takes place aboard what ship?

Which trailblazer was the first white man to see the Great Salt Lake?

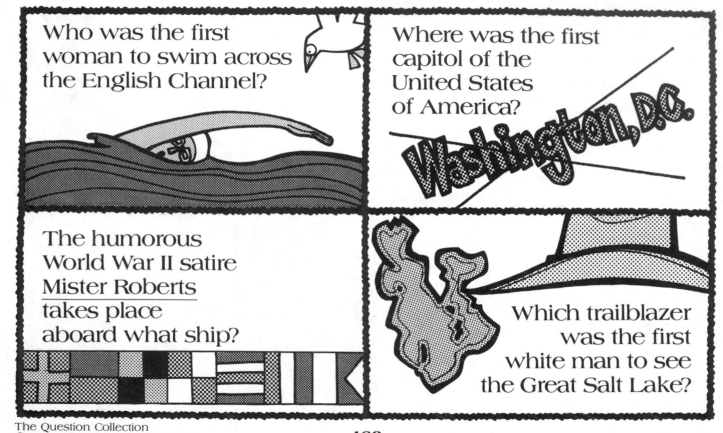

In which city is the Baseball Hall of Fame located?

For whom was F. Scott Fitzgerald named?

Name the Negro slave whose suit for citizenship as a free man went to the Supreme Court.

What was the secret effort to develop an atomic bomb called?

TOP SECRET

Who was the first secretary of the treasury?

Germany's sinking of what "unarmed" passenger liner caused the United States to enter World War I?

What romantic novel written by Benedict and Mary Freedman depicts pioneer life in Canada after the turn of the century?

Name the athlete who was the first American woman to win three gold medals in Olympic track and field competition.

Answer Key

Page 9
a. red, yellow, and blue
b. a tadpole
c. raisins
d. twelve

Page 10
a. an oak tree
b. a thermometer
c. Abraham Lincoln's
d. a calf

Page 11
a. prunes
b. the number 10
c. sixteen ounces
d. a fawn

Page 12
a. a dam
b. thirty-six inches
c. an atlas
d. the Mayflower

Page 13
a. the fifty states
b. Greece
c. "A Christmas Carol"
d. George Washington

Page 14
a. an island
b. Thomas Alva Edison
c. the Nile River
d. Rip Van Winkle

Page 15
a. an octagon
b. Paul Bunyan
c. Canada
d. Betsy Ross

Page 16
a. table salt
b. the mouth
c. the Pacific Ocean
d. Johnny Appleseed, who was born John Chapman

Page 17
a. George Washington's
b. purple
c. six points
d. bark

Page 18
a. five arms
b. the giraffe
c. a joint
d. four voices

Page 19
a. quintuplets
b. six legs
c. the number 5
d. He is your uncle.

Page 20
a. one hundred years
b. Thomas Jefferson's
c. Mexico
d. a tornado

The Question Collection
© 1988—The Learning Works, Inc.

Page 21
a. the thirteen original colonies
b. 1492
c. a genie
d. the bald eagle

Page 22
a. 2000 pounds
b. six sides
c. orange
d. a veterinarian

Page 23
a. Dr. Doolittle
b. a school
c. two pints
d. the Mississippi River

Page 24
a. four quarts
b. eyeglasses
c. Abraham Lincoln's
d. in the east

Page 25
a. gills
b. eight sides
c. Paris, France
d. He or she is your cousin.

Page 26
a. George Washington's
b. Independence Day
c. an octopus
d. a cub

Page 27
a. a rooster or a cock
b. twenty-four hours or one day
c. ice
d. 365 days

Page 28
a. constellations
b. black
c. a bird
d. H_2O

Page 29
a. in Sherwood Forest
b. irrigation
c. Benjamin Franklin
d. Hawaii

Page 30
a. in Houston, Texas
b. kayak
c. George Washington
d. Peter Pan

Page 31
a. peninsula
b. Alexander Graham Bell
c. Casey
d. the Atlantic Ocean

Page 32
a. Sally Ride
b. France
c. Mount St. Helens
d. polio or poliomyelitis

Page 33
a. horseback riding
b. Gerald Ford
c. Herman Melville
d. the African bush elephant

Page 34
a. 366 days
b. the number 100
c. Jupiter
d. a hunting dog

Page 35
a. Carlsbad Caverns, in New Mexico
b. Dr. Watson
c. the Jungle Books
d. Charles A. Lindbergh

Page 36
a. a tidal wave or tsunami
b. autumn or fall
c. the blue whale
d. its orbit

Page 37
a. the Panama Canal
b. Long John Silver
c. Sandra Day O'Connor
d. the esophagus

Page 38
a. the sum
b. three points
c. fossils
d. post meridiem

Page 39
a. Fern Arable
b. Hiroshima, Japan
c. Geraldine Ferraro
d. in Kitty Hawk, North Carolina

Page 40
a. fifty-two weeks
b. a joey
c. croquet
d. the product

Page 41
a. Walt Whitman
b. The Spirit of St. Louis
c. the site of a nuclear reactor
d. tea

Page 42
a. Wynken, Blynken, and Nod
b. the beaver
c. the moon
d. one hundred centimeters

Page 43
a. black
b. the sun
c. the cheetah
d. four sides

Page 44
a. seven continents
b. Babe
c. Philadelphia, Pennsylvania
d. a pentagon

Page 45
a. Will Rogers
b. lions
c. the Sahara
d. Theodore ("Teddy") Roosevelt

Page 46
a. the equator
b. the Arctic Ocean
c. a pair of silver skates
d. the Wright brothers, Orville and Wilbur

Page 47
a. three-fourths
b. Lyndon Johnson
c. Templeton
d. William Penn

Page 48
a. four years
b. Just So Stories
c. San Francisco, California
d. the Model T

Page 49
a. South Dakota
b. the Peace Corps
c. Neil A. Armstrong
d. Australia

Page 50
a. 98.6° F
b. gravity
c. a calf
d. tides

Page 51
a. Vietcong
b. because light travels faster than sound
c. the circumference
d. Beth

Page 52
a. 1776
b. Ebenezer Scrooge
c. Kennedy Space Center in Cape Canaveral, Florida
d. the Titanic

Page 53
a. Robinson
b. diamond
c. in the arm or elbow
d. four

Page 54
a. the diameter
b. the quotient
c. Judy Blume
d. on the left

Page 55
a. chlorophyll
b. the nucleus
c. humidity
d. Becky Thatcher

Page 56
a. True Grit
b. mercury
c. Franklin D. Roosevelt
d. at the inaugural ceremony or at the inauguration

Page 57
a. the Erie Canal
b. Thomas Jefferson
c. the U.S. Supreme Court
d. a raven

Page 58
a. Paul Revere
b. Asia
c. six sides
d. Wilbur

Page 59
a. Brazil
b. ante meridiem
c. golf
d. the difference or the remainder

Page 60
a. evergreen
b. a lion
c. a right angle
d. Friar Tuck

Page 61
a. Ronald Reagan
b. Willy Wonka
c. the radius
d. eight pints

Page 62
a. Martin Luther King, Jr.
b. Amelia Earhart
c. Amy
d. District of Columbia

Page 63
a. on a Civil War battlefield that was being dedicated as a cemetery in Gettysburg, Pennsylvania
b. Lilliput
c. two terms
d. the dust bowl

Page 64
a. solid, liquid, and gas
b. the Democratic party and the Republican party
c. England or Great Britain
d. Rhett Butler

Page 65
a. a barometer
b. Lee Harvey Oswald
c. the California condor
d. astronomy

Page 66
a. Houston, Texas
b. a Golden Ticket in a Wonka candy bar
c. ten years
d. Winston Churchill

Page 67
a. a biography
b. Mars
c. ligaments
d. sixteen cups

Page 68
a. South Vietnam
b. twenty-six miles
c. vertebrates
d. Harriet Beecher Stowe

Page 69
a. an isthmus
b. Jo
c. Benjamin Franklin
d. Theodore Roosevelt

Page 70
a. 360 degrees
b. origami
c. a satellite
d. fables

Page 71
a. June
b. the gingham dog and the calico cat
c. Jupiter
d. the crocodile

Page 72
a. the Emancipation Proclamation
b. vitamin D
c. the adverb
d. E. B. White

Page 73
a. Eli Whitney
b. an acute angle
c. Theodore Roosevelt
d. In God We Trust

Page 74
a. coonhounds
b. Mount Everest
c. Ronald Reagan
d. Samuel F. B. Morse

Page 75
a. a tributary
b. Helen Keller
c. Thomas Alva Edison
d. Mount McKinley

Page 76
a. the village smithy or the village blacksmith
b. a meridian or line of longitude
c. Yellowstone, in Wyoming
d. Argentina

Page 77
a. 100°C or 212°F
b. graphite
c. the gestapo, or secret police, of Nazi Germany
d. Neil A. Armstrong

Page 78
a. John Adams
b. Michelangelo
c. in Athens, Greece
d. Hans Christian Andersen

Page 79
a. Alaska
b. Ford's Theatre
c. France
d. Gone With the Wind

Page 80
a. the wisdom teeth
b. doughboys
c. Jim
d. every four years

Page 81
a. tooth enamel
b. Patrick Henry
c. in Sleepy Hollow
d. 365 days or one year

Page 82
a. Liberty Island
b. The Grapes of Wrath
c. Spain
d. in the eye

Page 83
a. at Promontory Point, Utah
b. George Washington, Thomas Jefferson, Abraham Lincoln, and Theodore Roosevelt
c. a lion
d. Chicago

Page 84
a. Old North Church
b. the Great Depression
c. the executive, the legislative and the judicial
d. The Time Machine

Page 85
a. E. B. White
b. barter
c. fireside chats
d. the Union of Soviet Socialist Republics

Page 86
a. the number 1000
b. migration
c. the Richter scale
d. Hannibal, Missouri

Page 87
a. two senators
b. Pluto
c. Valley Forge, Pennsylvania
d. Romeo and Juliet

Page 88
a. Mr. Hyde
b. the Declaration of Independence
c. Massachusetts
d. Alfred Joyce Kilmer, who is known simply as Joyce Kilmer

Page 89
a. Moby Dick
b. John Adams
c. the source
d. Benjamin Franklin, under the pseudonym of Richard Saunders

Page 90
a. sunspots
b. General Robert E. Lee
c. December
d. 0°C or 32°F

Page 91
a. Lake Michigan
b. the adjective
c. every ten years
d. William F. ("Buffalo Bill") Cody

Page 92
a. Venus
b. The Prince and the Pauper
c. six players
d. Jefferson Davis

Page 93
a. France
b. the hummingbird
c. Golda Meir
d. eleven players

Page 94
a. Alan B. Shepard, Jr.
b. "Old Hickory"
c. at Pearl Harbor, a U.S. naval base on the south coast of Oahu in the Hawaiian Islands
d. Sherlock Holmes

Page 95
a. an autobiography
b. Miami, Florida
c. Halley's comet
d. molting

Page 96
a. Erie, Huron, Michigan, Ontario, Superior
b. Kon-Tiki
c. an albatross
d. Sacagawea

Page 97
a. 29½ days or about a month
b. Louisa May Alcott
c. nonfiction
d. Martha Dandridge Custis

Page 98
a. a dog
b. twenty-four
c. General Ulysses S. Grant
d. a gaggle

Page 99
a. Henry Hudson
b. Philadelphia, Pennsylvania
c. Norman Rockwell
d. The Yearling

Page 100
a. a parallel or line of latitude
b. Little Men
c. Francis Scott Key
d. Sequoia, in California

Page 101
a. A. A. Milne
b. Leonardo da Vinci
c. Mark Spitz
d. Mercury

Page 102
a. the peregrine falcon
b. the Rough Riders
c. Hiawatha
d. spring

Page 103
a. in Dallas, Texas, on November 22, 1963
b. the Pony Express
c. deciduous
d. Lilies of the Field

Page 104
a. pointillism
b. Italy
c. the League of Nations
d. Candlestick Park

Page 105
a. the avocado
b. He is a lawyer.
c. the Alamo
d. a paleontologist

Page 106
a. Silent Spring
b. a metronome
c. Mars
d. George Washington

Page 107
a. Russian cosmonaut Yuri Gagarin
b. Herbert Hoover
c. a pearl
d. nine

Page 108
a. the National Archives in Washington, D.C.
b. John Paul Jones
c. carpetbaggers
d. eighty-eight

Page 109
a. Italian navigator Amerigo Vespucci
b. stalagmites
c. two-thirds
d. December 7, 1941

Page 110
a. Vincent Van Gogh
b. He is a sled dog.
c. Franklin Delano Roosevelt
d. Howard Hughes

Page 111
a. Carry Nation
b. Sooners
c. Jules Verne
d. the Axis nations or the Axis powers

Page 112
a. Martin Luther King, Jr.
b. Venus
c. the spoils system
d. Noah Webster

Page 113
a. Delaware
b. Joseph Stalin
c. stalactites
d. 93 million miles

Page 114
a. the number 50
b. igneous, metamorphic, and sedimentary
c. George Washington
d. in the ear

Page 115
a. the Milky Way galaxy
b. Lafayette
c. her father
d. the femur or thigh-bone

The Question Collection
© 1988—The Learning Works, Inc.

Page 116
a. the Monroe Doctrine
b. rural Mississippi
c. an obtuse angle
d. meteorologists

Page 117
a. The Martian Chronicles
b. Russia
c. women's suffrage
d. black, yellow, green, red, and blue

Page 118
a. John F. Kennedy
b. lodestone
c. fourteen nights and days or two weeks
d. Philadelphia, Pennsylvania

Page 119
a. evolution
b. St. Augustine, Florida, which was founded in September 1565
c. the Sears Tower in Chicago
d. the widow Douglas

Page 120
a. Meriwether Lewis and William Clark
b. fencing
c. a bone in the lower leg
d. Simon Legree

Page 121
a. Benedict Arnold
b. the Stanley Cup
c. Sequoia, in California
d. He does not have a voice.

Page 122
a. Salem, Massachusetts
b. dry ice
c. 5,280 feet
d. "If"

Page 123
a. Edgar Degas
b. Hernando De Soto
c. the New Deal
d. Tracy Austin

Page 124
a. John Glenn
b. Old Yeller
c. John Adams
d. Nuremberg

Page 125
a. Woodrow Wilson
b. Pluto
c. Ernest H. Shepard
d. Mark Twain

Page 126
a. Of Mice and Men
b. the decathlon
c. a musical instrument
d. D Day

Page 127
a. the troposphere
b. the fineness, or purity, of gold
c. four
d. the Spanish-American War

Page 128
a. invertebrates
b. F. Scott Fitzgerald
c. France
d. refraction

Page 129
a. soccer
b. Thomas Jefferson
c. Grant Wood
d. the crust

Page 130
a. Canada
b. Captain John Smith
c. cartographer
d. "A Visit from St. Nicholas"

Page 131
a. coins
b. the Bill of Rights
c. "The Man without a Country"
d. an archaeologist

Page 132
a. Uncle Remus, in Uncle Remus by Joel Chandler Harris
b. two points
c. zoologists
d. at the courthouse in Appomattox, Virginia

Page 133
a. The Clan of the Cave Bear
b. suffrage or the right to vote
c. at Arlington National Cemetery in Virginia
d. the North African ostrich

Page 134
a. the stamen
b. "The Fall of the House of Usher"
c. Roanoke Island, off the coast of North Carolina in Croatoan Sound
d. the epidermis

Page 135
a. Booker T. Washington
b. Ichabod Crane
c. stamps
d. the Oregon Trail

Page 136
a. twenty years
b. the Chisholm Trail
c. the Lincoln-Douglas debates
d. Katrina Van Tassel

Page 137
a. Captains Courageous
b. two hundred bones
c. Mercury, with an average speed in orbit of 107,030 miles per hour
d. Tecumseh

Page 138
a. Christian Huygens
b. Calaveras County, California
c. Dicey
d. Hawaii Volcanoes National Park

The Question Collection
© 1988—The Learning Works, Inc.

Page 139
a. the reticulated python of Southeast Asia, Indochina, and the Philippines
b. the Ozarks
c. Venus
d. It made segregation of students in public schools illegal.

Page 140
a. lithosphere
b. James Madison
c. Lennie Small
d. three

Page 141
a. December 22
b. the Dead Sea
c. nitrogen
d. at Yorktown, Virginia

Page 142
a. Matthew Calbraith Perry
b. 16 pounds
c. the hummingbird
d. the jawbone of a whale

Page 143
a. London, England
b. General Dwight D. Eisenhower
c. Sitting Bull and Crazy Horse
d. Santiago

Page 144
a. the Clermont
b. Polaris
c. Garth Williams
d. Nat Turner

Page 145
a. San Francisco, California
b. Powhatan
c. aboard a British ship near Fort McHenry in 1814
d. Stranger with My Face

Page 146
a. on the California side of the White Mountains in the Inyo National Forest
b. the high jump
c. Francisco Vasques de Coronado
d. Andy Warhol

Page 147
a. Tippecanoe and Tyler, Too
b. Minnehaha, which means "Laughing Water"
c. The Chocolate War
d. Samuel de Champlain

Page 148
a. James Oglethorpe
b. Georgia O'Keefe
c. Mildred ("Babe") Didrikson Zaharias
d. Count Vronsky

Page 149
a. Theodore Roosevelt
b. James McNeill Whistler
c. Proxima Centauri
d. Poker Flat

Page 150
a. Uncas
b. Vincent Van Gogh
c. in Akron, Ohio
d. President Andrew Johnson

Page 151
a. Jamestown, Virginia
b. Venus
c. George Herman Ruth
d. Nautilus

Page 152
a. Hideki Tojo
b. thunder and lightning
c. Frances Perkins
d. Australia

Page 153
a. Everglades, in Florida
b. a rodeo accident
c. the prime meridian
d. Alfred Nobel

Page 154
a. the Paris Exposition of 1889
b. copper and tin
c. General Charles Cornwallis
d. the Open Door Policy

Page 155
a. John Winthrop
b. General John J. Pershing
c. the St. Lawrence Seaway
d. Charles Lutwidge Dodgson

Page 156
a. "Old Ironsides"
b. the Bataan Death March
c. The Heart Is a Lonely Hunter
d. Sequoyah

Page 157
a. John Jay
b. Bellipotent
c. Priscilla
d. Chief Joseph

Page 158
a. Gunpowder
b. the stratosphere
c. the mountain gorilla
d. the Red Baron

Page 159
a. Kit Carson
b. the Wyeth family
c. a turkey
d. Thomas Paine

Page 160
a. the Marshall Plan
b. William Henry Harrison
c. Miles Standish
d. at Fort Sumter in South Carolina

Page 161
a. Henry Wadsworth Longfellow
b. the battle of Wounded Knee
c. Thurgood Marshall
d. June 21

Page 162
a. Cyrus McCormick
b. the Pequod
c. Yellowstone, in Wyoming
d. William Bradford

Page 163
a. Yosemite, in California
b. Explorer I
c. Tom Canty
d. Sutter's Mill on the American River

Page 164
a. Aron
b. Grover Cleveland
c. twelve seconds
d. Francis Bellamy

Page 165
a. seventeen
b. the U.S.S. Maine
c. Elias Howe
d. 24

Page 166
a. Boulder Dam
b. Andrew Jackson
c. Aaron Burr
d. Virginia

Page 167
a. the Trail of Tears
b. Sinclair Lewis
c. John Roosevelt Robinson, who was also known as Jackie Robinson
d. UNIVAC I

Page 168
a. Gertrude Ederle
b. in New York City
c. the U.S.S. Reluctant
d. Jim Bridger

Page 169
a. Cooperstown, New York
b. Francis Scott Key. Fitzgerald's full name was Francis Scott Key Fitzgerald.
c. Dred Scott
d. the Manhattan Project

Page 170
a. Alexander Hamilton
b. the Lusitania
c. Mrs. Mike
d. Wilma Rudolph